333.95
OCO

O'Connell, Kim A.

The Galapagos
  penguin.

47311

$25.26

DATE			

BAKER & TAYLOR

ENDANGERED AND THREATENED ANIMALS

THE GALÁPAGOS PENGUIN

A MyReportLinks.com Book

Kim A. O'Connell

MyReportLinks.com Books

an imprint of

Enslow Publishers, Inc.

Box 398, 40 Industrial Road
Berkeley Heights, NJ 07922
USA

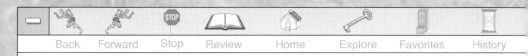
47311

MyReportLinks.com Books, an imprint of Enslow Publishers, Inc. MyReportLinks® is a registered trademark of Enslow Publishers, Inc.

Library of Congress Cataloging-in-Publication Data

O'Connell, Kim A.
  The Galapagos penguin / Kim A. O'Connell.
    p. cm. — (Endangered and threatened animals)
  Includes bibliographical references (p.   ).
  ISBN 0-7660-5063-7
  1. Penguins—Galapagos Islands—Juvenile literature. 2. Endangered species—Galapagos Islands—Juvenile literature. I. Title. II. Series.
  QL696.S473O29 2005
  333.95'847—dc22

                                                                                          2004009826

Printed in the United States of America

10 9 8 7 6 5 4 3 2 1

To Our Readers:
Through the purchase of this book, you and your library gain access to the Report Links that specifically back up this book.
The Publisher will provide access to the Report Links that back up this book and will keep these Report Links up to date on **www.myreportlinks.com** for five years from the book's first publication date.
We have done our best to make sure all Internet addresses in this book were active and appropriate when we went to press. However, the author and the Publisher have no control over, and assume no liability for, the material available on those Internet sites or on other Web sites they may link to. The usage of the MyReportLinks.com Books Web site is subject to the terms and conditions stated on the Usage Policy Statement on **www.myreportlinks.com**.
A password may be required to access the Report Links that back up this book. The password is found on the bottom of page 4 of this book.
Any comments or suggestions can be sent by e-mail to comments@myreportlinks.com or to the address on the back cover.

Photo Credits: © Corel Corporation, pp. 3, 10, 11, 13, 20, 26, 32, 34, 38, 41, 43; © Dr. Robert Rothman, Department of Biological Sciences, Rochester Institute of Technology, pp. 17, 21, 22, 39; © The Charles Darwin Foundation for the Galápagos Islands, p. 14; Galapagos Conservation Trust, p. 31; Galápagos Geology on the Web, p. 36; John Bavaro, p. 18; Marcus Martin (www.photobirder.com), pp. 1, 3; Marine Science, p. 28; MyReportLinks.com Books, p. 4; Penguin Taxon Advisory Group, p. 30; Swiss Association of Friends of the Galapagos Islands, p. 24.

Cover Photo: Galápagos penguin on Isabela Island, Marcus Martin (www.photobirder.com).

Contents

MyReportLinks.com Books
Great Books, Great Links, Great for Research!

The Internet sites listed on the next five pages can save you hours of research time. These Internet sites—we call them "Report Links"—are constantly changing, but we keep them up to date on our Web site.

Give it a try! Type http://www.myreportlinks.com into your browser, click on the series title, then the book title, and scroll down to the Report Links listed for this book.

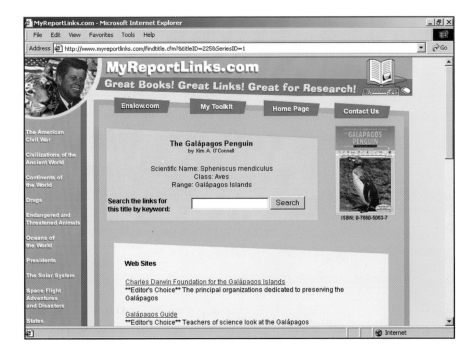

The Report Links will bring you to great source documents, photographs, and illustrations. MyReportLinks.com Books save you time, feature Report Links that are kept up to date, and make report writing easier than ever!

Please see "To Our Readers" on the copyright page for important information about this book, the MyReportLinks.com Web site, and the Report Links that back up this book.

Please enter **EGA1773** if asked for a password.

Report Links

The Internet sites described below can be accessed at
http://www.myreportlinks.com

*EDITOR'S CHOICE

▶ **Charles Darwin Foundation for the Galápagos Islands**
The Charles Darwin Foundation for the Galápagos Islands and the
Galápagos National Park are responsible for protecting the unique plants
and animals of the Galápagos Islands of Ecuador. Learn more about the
important work the foundation does.

Link to this Internet site from http://www.myreportlinks.com

*EDITOR'S CHOICE

▶ **Galápagos Guide**
This NTSA (National Teachers of Science Association) site offers varied
and interesting information about the islands of the Galápagos and some
of the fascinating wildlife found there.

Link to this Internet site from http://www.myreportlinks.com

*EDITOR'S CHOICE

▶ **Galápagos Islands**
With a rich history, an interesting topography, and unique wildlife, the
islands that make up the Galápagos are a fascinating subject. Read more
about the Ecuadorian archipelago and why its ecosystems are threatened.

Link to this Internet site from http://www.myreportlinks.com

*EDITOR'S CHOICE

▶ **Galápagos Penguin**
Interesting facts about Galápagos penguins, including feeding behavior,
reproduction, and population numbers are included in this site, which
offers a link to additional photographs of this small marine species.

Link to this Internet site from http://www.myreportlinks.com

*EDITOR'S CHOICE

▶ **Galápagos National Park**
The Galápagos National Park, dedicated to protecting the unique species
of the islands, covers most of the archipelago. The park service's site offers
news, views, and a video clip.

Link to this Internet site from http://www.myreportlinks.com

*EDITOR'S CHOICE

▶ **Galápagos Geology**
This site looks at the geology of the Galápagos Islands, a volcanic island
group in the Pacific. Also included is information about the islands'
history, including visits from pirates, whalers, and Charles Darwin.

Link to this Internet site from http://www.myreportlinks.com

Report Links

The Internet sites described below can be accessed at
http://www.myreportlinks.com

Charles Darwin Foundation, Inc.

This conservation foundation (not that same as the Charles Darwin
Foundation for the Galápagos Islands) began as part of a Smithsonian
Institution trust fund. Its Web site includes news about efforts to protect
the islands' species.

Link to this Internet site from http://www.myreportlinks.com

The Effect of El Niño in Galápagos on the Marine Fish and Birds

As this site describes, El Niño is a disruption of the atmospheric system in
the tropical Pacific Ocean that affects climate around the world. It has had
a devastating effect on some Galápagos species, including the penguins.

Link to this Internet site from http://www.myreportlinks.com

Endangered Species Information, U.S. Fish & Wildlife Service

The United States Fish and Wildlife Service lists threatened and endangered
animals and plants worldwide. This USFWS page offers links to the database
in which those species, including the Galápagos penguin, are listed.

Link to this Internet site from http://www.myreportlinks.com

The Flightless Seabirds

The Galápagos penguin is the only species of penguin that lives near the
equator. The cold Humboldt Current provides waters cold enough for them
to survive. At this site, learn more about these flightless birds.

Link to this Internet site from http://www.myreportlinks.com

Galápagos

An IMAX documentary explores the Galápagos Islands, an archipelago of
nineteen islands and forty-two islets situated six hundred miles west of
mainland Ecuador. Check out the Deep Sea Search game, and view a video
clip from the film.

Link to this Internet site from http://www.myreportlinks.com

The Galápagos Conservation Trust

The Galápagos Conservation Trust is a British organization that works
closely with other conservation organizations to protect Galápagos Islands
wildlife. At the organization's site, read about ongoing efforts to protect the
Galápagos penguin.

Link to this Internet site from http://www.myreportlinks.com

Report Links

The Internet sites described below can be accessed at
http://www.myreportlinks.com

▶ Galápagos Islands

This WWF site profiles the islands of the Galápagos. Although only five
of the islands are inhabited by people, tourism is hugely important to the
local economy. Learn more about the unique ecosystem and the diversity
of species that call it home.

Link to this Internet site from http://www.myreportlinks.com

▶ Galápagos Penguin

Dr. Richard Rothman, an American biologist, has long been fascinated
with the wildlife of the Galápagos, including its penguins. His site offers
a look at these birds as well as a history of the islands and interesting
descriptions of other native wildlife.

Link to this Internet site from http://www.myreportlinks.com

▶ Galápagos Penguin: Scientific Name: *Spheniscus mendiculus*

The Galápagos penguin is part of the Spheniscidae family of penguins,
which includes the Humboldt, Magellanic, and African penguins. This
site looks at the challenges faced by Galápagos penguins.

Link to this Internet site from http://www.myreportlinks.com

▶ Impacts of El Niño on Galápagos Penguins' Body Condition and Movement

During a prolonged El Niño, Galápagos penguins have become sick,
stopped breeding, and even starved to death because of depleted fish
stocks. Learn about this phenomenon and its effect on Galápagos penguins.

Link to this Internet site from http://www.myreportlinks.com

▶ International Penguin Conservation Work Group: Galápagos Penguin

This site from a group dedicated to penguin conservation includes a page
about Galápagos penguins.

Link to this Internet site from http://www.myreportlinks.com

▶ Interview With Dr. Dee Boersma

This site from the University of Washington provides an interview with
Dr. Dee Boersma. A biologist on the university's faculty, Dr. Boersma is
an expert on penguins who is concerned about the future of the
Galápagos penguin.

Link to this Internet site from http://www.myreportlinks.com

Report Links

➤ The Internet sites described below can be accessed at
http://www.myreportlinks.com

Into the Abyss?
Overfishing, pollution, climate changes that lead to food shortages, the
introduction of alien species, and human disturbances are just some of the
threats to penguins' survival. At this site, learn more about these threats.

Link to this Internet site from http://www.myreportlinks.com

IUCN Red List of Threatened Species
The IUCN–World Conservation Union Red List is a searchable database
of the world's endangered animals and plants. A summary of each species
includes information on habitats and major threats.

Link to this Internet site from http://www.myreportlinks.com

New Hope for Sensitive Sea Areas
This article praises action taken by the International Maritime Organization
for its designation of the Galápagos Islands as a Particularly Sensitive Sea Area
(PSSA). This designation requires ships to take special care when navigating
through such areas.

Link to this Internet site from http://www.myreportlinks.com

No More Pigs on Santiago
Feral pigs once posed a threat to Galápagos penguins on Santiago Island,
but the pigs have now been successfully eradicated. This site from a charitable
organization known as the Swiss Association of Friends of the Galápagos
Islands tells how this was accomplished.

Link to this Internet site from http://www.myreportlinks.com

Penguin
Defenders of Wildlife is a conservation organization dedicated to protecting
all wild animals in their natural habitats. This page from their site for kids
offers a brief overview of facts about penguins.

Link to this Internet site from http://www.myreportlinks.com

Penguins: A SeaWorld Education Department Resource
This SeaWorld site presents a comprehensive look at the world's penguin
species. Topics include physical characteristics, diet and eating habits,
conservation, and much more.

Link to this Internet site from http://www.myreportlinks.com

▶**Penguins on Thin Ice**
The world's penguin species, who live in diverse habitats, eat different
foods, and vary widely in size, behavior, and number, are profiled in
this site.

Link to this Internet site from http://www.myreportlinks.com

▶*The Origin of Species*
Charles Darwin's observations of the animals on the Galápagos had a great
effect on his theories of natural selection, the subject of his famous work
The Origin of Species. A full-text version of that important book is
available at this site.

Link to this Internet site from http://www.myreportlinks.com

▶*The Voyage of the* Beagle
Charles Darwin's account of his voyage aboard the *Beagle* is available in
full at this site. Chapter Seventeen includes Darwin's observations of the
species he encountered on the Galápagos archipelago.

Link to this Internet site from http://www.myreportlinks.com

▶**Unique Galápagos Seabirds Endangered by *Jessica* Oil Spill**
In 2001, a tanker named *Jessica* ran aground in the waters off the Galápagos,
pouring 190,000 gallons of diesel into the sea, with some of it reaching
several islands. Read more about this accident and the consequences for
wildlife on the islands.

Link to this Internet site from http://www.myreportlinks.com

▶**Why Conserve Birds?**
Birds are indicators of an ecosystem's stability and health. Without birds,
many plants would not be pollinated. At this site, learn more about the
importance of birds, including penguins, to our planet's survival.

Link to this Internet site from http://www.myreportlinks.com

▶**The World of Penguins**
The more we learn about penguins, the more likely we are to ensure that
these birds will be protected from extinction. This PBS site offers lots of
information about penguins and includes a video.

Link to this Internet site from http://www.myreportlinks.com

Scientific Name

Spheniscus mendiculus

Habitat/Range

Range is limited to the Galápagos Islands off the coast of Ecuador.

Average Weight

4 to 5 pounds
(1.8 to 2.3 kilograms)

Average Length

20 to 24 inches
(51 to 61 centimeters)

Life Span

Most adult penguins live from three to twenty-five years.

Status

The Galápagos penguin is the only penguin species listed as endangered under the United States Endangered Species Act.

Coloration

Adults: Black wings and upper parts and white under parts, with an irregular black line running from the upper breast down to the tail. Black face with a white line running through the eye down the cheeks and across the throat.

Immature: Generally gray and lacks distinctive head and body markings of adults.

Breeding Season

Breeding occurs throughout the year, depending upon available food, which is dependent upon water temperatures.

Incubation Period

Forty to forty-two days

Threats to Survival

Starvation due to changing water temperatures caused by El Niño weather events; habitat loss; introduced predators; illegal fishing practices; pollution; and disease.

Penguins—and an Island Paradise —at Risk

Six hundred miles off the coast of Ecuador, the rocky islands of the Galápagos rise from the Pacific Ocean. These islands, formed from volcanoes, are surrounded by the faraway horizon.

As volcanic islands go, the Galápagos Islands are fairly "young," with the oldest islands only a few million years old. Some Galápagos volcanoes are still active, occasionally spewing lava that continues to add to these islands' rocky shapes. Today, this archipelago, or group of islands, is made up of thirteen large islands, six small islands, and dozens of other small islets and rocky outcrops.

Chapter 1

▶ Incredible Plants and Animals

Isolated from the mainland of South America, the Galápagos Islands are home to plant and animal species found nowhere else on Earth. These endemic, or

◀ The giant Galápagos tortoise gave the island archipelago its name.

native, species include about half the islands' birds, one third of the plants, and nearly all of the reptiles. One of those reptiles—the giant Galápagos tortoise—gives the archipelago its name: *Galápago* is Spanish for "tortoise."

Some wildlife experts estimate that the islands are home to three quarters of a million seabirds, including boobies, pelicans, cormorants, and frigate birds. The islands' waters are also home to a full range of marine life, from microscopic sea creatures to large whales. Unfortunately, it is precisely *because* these islands are home to such an incredible variety of wildlife that people have made the Galápagos a tourist destination. And within the last thirty years, more people have moved to some of the islands. They have brought their domestic animals with them, created waste, and competed for food in the form of fishing. All of these things affect the islands' native species, who for centuries lived without interference from humans.

One of the native species most affected by these changes is the tiny Galápagos penguin, the third-smallest penguin species and the only one found breeding on both sides of the equator. Although this bird is flightless, it is a great swimmer, known for "flying" through the water, diving after fish, its main food. Galápagos penguins once flourished in their remote island paradise, but today only a few thousand of these birds remain.

▶ Why They Are at Risk

With a shrinking population and limited range, the Galápagos penguin is listed as endangered by the United States Fish and Wildlife Service. Threats to the penguin include habitat loss, illegal fishing practices, and increased tourism to the islands. In addition, introduced animals such

▲ *A tiny Galápagos penguin on one of the islands' lava rocks. These small marine mammals once flourished in the Galápagos, but nature and humans have combined to diminish their population.*

as rats, cats, and dogs attack penguin eggs and penguin chicks. One of the deadliest threats comes from a natural event known as El Niño. El Niño is a recurring flow of warmer-than-usual surface water from the Pacific Ocean that travels toward and along the western coast of South America. This heated-up current prevents nutrient-rich colder water from reaching the coast and results in weather patterns that affect not only the region but also the entire planet. For the Galápagos penguin, El Niño events have brought serious consequences because fish cannot survive in the warmer waters, and it is in these waters that the penguins find their food. An El Niño event in 1982 and 1983 was particularly damaging to the Galápagos penguin population, reducing it by more than 70 percent.

"The food shortage around the Galápagos Islands was so acute," said Dr. P. Dee Boersma, a biologist from the University of Washington and a penguin specialist, "that reproduction stopped and a lot of adult birds starved to death."[1] Dr. Boersma fears that increases in the number of El Niño events, combined with other threats (mostly introduced by humans through tourism and fishing), could force this species into extinction.

▷ Saving Galápagos Penguins

Because of these threats and low population numbers, individuals and organizations are working to protect the

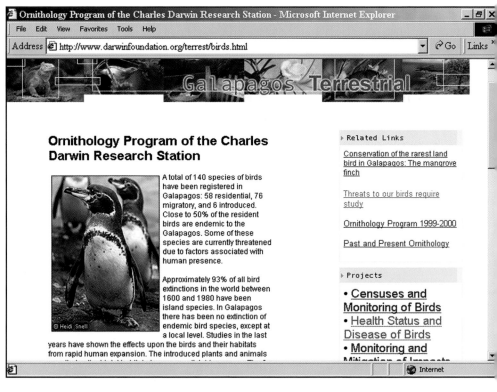

Ornithology Program of the Charles Darwin Research Station - Microsoft Internet Explorer

File   Edit   View   Favorites   Tools   Help

Address ｜ http://www.darwinfoundation.org/terrest/birds.html   Go | Links

Galapagos Terrestrial

Ornithology Program of the Charles Darwin Research Station

© Heidi Snell

A total of 140 species of birds have been registered in Galapagos: 58 residential, 76 migratory, and 6 introduced. Close to 50% of the resident birds are endemic to the Galapagos. Some of these species are currently threatened due to factors associated with human presence.

Approximately 93% of all bird extinctions in the world between 1600 and 1980 have been island species. In Galapagos there has been no extinction of endemic bird species, except at a local level. Studies in the last years have shown the effects upon the birds and their habitats from rapid human expansion. The introduced plants and animals

▸ Related Links

Conservation of the rarest land bird in Galapagos: The mangrove finch

Threats to our birds require study

Ornithology Program 1999-2000

Past and Present Ornithology

▸ Projects

• **Censuses and Monitoring of Birds**
• **Health Status and Disease of Birds**
• **Monitoring and**

Internet

The Charles Darwin Research Station is dedicated to the conservation of the islands' penguin population as well as the archipelago's other animal and plant species.

Galápagos penguin in its only habitat. That habitat is contained within the Galápagos National Park and the Galápagos Marine Reserve, which cover 97 percent of the islands' land area and all the ocean within 40 miles (64 kilometers) of the archipelago's coast.

The Charles Darwin Foundation, dedicated to the conservation of the Galápagos ecosystems, operates the Charles Darwin Research Station on the islands. Its team of more than two hundred scientists, educators, volunteers, and students come from around the world to do research and provide monitoring of the islands' unique animal and plant species. The Research Station carries out a yearly census of the penguin population in the Galápagos Islands and tags penguins to get more accurate numbers of the species' decline over time. Other organizations, including the Galápagos Conservation Trust, based in Great Britain, and the WWF (formerly known as the World Wildlife Fund), are also involved in conservation efforts. Following the dramatic El Niño events of 1982 and 1983, the population of Galápagos penguins has remained relatively stable. But if the Galápagos penguin population is to thrive, the effects of humans on the islands' native species will need to be controlled.

Chapter 2 ▶

Island Natives: Special Characteristics

The Galápagos were first discovered in 1535 by a Spanish priest named Tomás de Berlanga, who wrote about the tortoises and iguanas he found there. Since then, various groups of humans—from pirates and whalers to scientists, conservationists, and immigrants from around the world—have come to these islands for food, fact-finding, or fortune. Ecuador annexed the islands in 1832 and has retained control ever since. During World War II, the United States established an air base on Baltra Island for the defense of the Panama Canal. Unfortunately, land iguanas on the island were used for target practice, leading to the species' extinction.

Today, visitors to the Galápagos are most likely to be tourists. The most famous visitor to the Galápagos, however, was Charles Darwin.

▷ Natural Selection

In 1835, English naturalist Charles Darwin was in the fourth year of a five-year research cruise aboard the HMS *Beagle,* a ship that had been traveling along the coast of South America. Moving north from Chile, the ship made a stop at the Galápagos Islands. At first, Darwin was not impressed by what he saw. The marine iguanas sunning themselves on the rocky shores were "hideous-looking creatures," Darwin wrote in his diary. "The black rocks, heated by the rays of the vertical sun like a stove, give to the air a close and sultry feeling," he noted.[1]

Tools   Search   Notes   Discuss

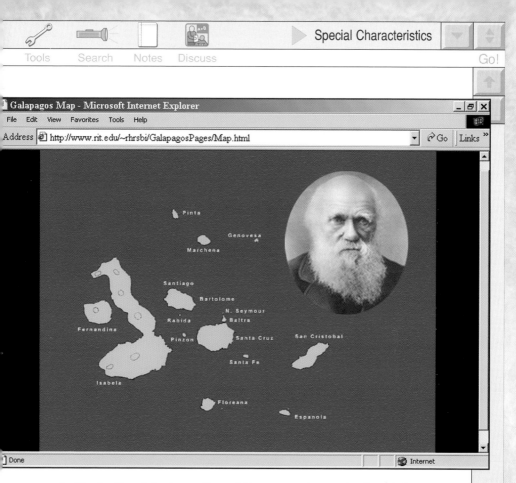

Galapagos Map - Microsoft Internet Explorer

File   Edit   View   Favorites   Tools   Help

Address http://www.rit.edu/~rhrsbi/GalapagosPages/Map.html   Go   Links

Pinta

Genovesa

Marchena

Santiago

Bartolome

N. Seymour

Rabida   Baltra

Fernandina

Pinzon   Santa Cruz   San Cristobal

Santa Fe

Isabela

Floreana

Espanola

Done   Internet

▲ *Charles Darwin's observations of the many unique animals and plants he found on the Galápagos Islands helped him to come up with the theory of natural selection.*

It was not long before Darwin began to appreciate the strange plants and wildlife that he saw in the Galápagos. He traveled from island to island, noticing that the animals were quite different from those found on the mainland. He was amazed by the islands' giant tortoises, large hawks, and small finches. After returning home to England, Darwin began to form a theory about evolution, or the process of how plant and animal species develop and change over time. In 1859, Darwin published *The Origin of Species,* in which he explained his theory of natural selection. According to the theory, species develop variations that help them to survive and reproduce, which are then passed down through offspring, generation after generation. This promotes what has sometimes been called "survival of the fittest." It is generally agreed that Darwin's experiences on the Galápagos helped him to form his theory.

▶ A Place for Penguins

One of the many species that has evolved and adapted to the environment of these volcanic islands on the equator is the Galápagos penguin. Although this penguin shares many characteristics with other penguins, it also has developed special features to survive in the hot equatorial sun.

Most of the world's seventeen penguin species live far south in the Southern Hemisphere, breeding in Antarctica and along the coasts of South America, South Africa, and Australia. These seabirds cannot fly, and they

Distinctive white band extends from the eye to underneath the chin.

Longer and more slender bill than other penguins.

Their chests feature a black band in inverted horseshoe shape.

Their black coats help them blend naturally into the surrounding black lava rocks.

Both flippers and feet aid in swimming.

◀ Galápagos penguins can "fly" through the water at tremendous speeds.

often look awkward waddling along on their stubby legs. Underwater, however, penguins can paddle and dive gracefully, searching for their next meal. Penguins have black backs and white bellies, which help to camouflage them when they are swimming. Viewed from above, their dark backs blend in with the ocean, but from underneath, their white bellies are hard to spot when sunlight is pouring down from the sky. This characteristic is known as countershading.

Penguins come in all sizes, with markings on their heads and bodies that help to distinguish them. The largest penguin species is the emperor penguin, which weighs up to 100 pounds (45 kilograms) when it is at its fattest and ready to molt all its feathers. By contrast, the smallest species, the little blue penguin, weighs only about two pounds (about one kilogram). The chinstrap penguin, which lives off the Antarctic Ocean coasts of South America and Africa, is named for the thin black band that encircles the lower part of its face like the strap of a helmet. Both the macaroni and the royal penguins sport bright yellow plumes on their heads. The most commonly thought-of penguin—whose black "coat" and white "shirt" resemble a tuxedo—is actually the Adélie penguin of Antarctica.

The Third Smallest Penguin

The Galápagos penguin is the third-smallest penguin species, standing only about 20 to 24 inches (51 to 61 centimeters) high and weighing 4 to 5 pounds (1.8 to 2.3 kilograms). Whereas most penguins are used to an environment that includes ice, snow, and frigid water, the Galápagos penguin makes its home on the equator. The Galápagos penguin's traditional range has been

▲ *Galápagos penguins, similar to Humboldt and Magellanic penguins in some of their markings, are much smaller than either. This pair was photographed on the islands' lava rocks, where their black coats help them to blend into their surroundings.*

Isabela and Fernandina islands, on the western side of the archipelago, where the water is cooler and food is often plentiful. These penguins do visit other islands, however, and are seen and occasionally breed on the islands of Santiago, Floreana, and Santa Cruz.

Scientists believe that the Galápagos penguin evolved from the similar Humboldt penguin species, which lives along the western coast of South America. A few Humboldts probably rode the cool and productive Peruvian current to make the lengthy swim to the Galápagos and managed to survive there. Over time, isolation and evolutionary changes created the species now known as the Galápagos penguin. The two species are similar in that both have a lot of naked skin around the bill because they live in hot environments, but Galápagos penguins are much smaller and have a longer, thinner bill than Humboldt penguins. The markings of the Galápagos penguin are like those of a Magellanic penguin with similar banding patterns.

When they are hot, Galápagos penguins hold their wings out at angles, allowing air to pass over and cool their bodies. In the hot sun and moist environment, penguin feathers easily become worn, and frequent molting protects the penguin from the cold ocean by giving it a new coat.

Breeding and Feeding

A day in the life of a Galápagos penguin might sound like a relaxing beach vacation. In the early morning or late

A Galápagos penguin diving for its dinner: Mullet and sardines make up most of the catch.

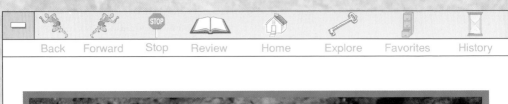

▲ *A juvenile Galápagos penguin on one of the islands' rocky coasts.*

afternoon, Galápagos penguins like to socialize and rest
on rocks warmed by the sun. When it gets hot, the penguins will move into coves and tree-shaded inlets.
Penguins can often be seen swimming among the roots of
tropical mangrove trees or along the shoreline in groups of
up to fifty birds or more. On the surface, penguins stay
half submerged, swimming in a lazy fashion. Underwater,
Galápagos penguins are all business, diving and searching
for the fish and shellfish that make up their diet.
Although the birds are usually fairly quiet, during breeding season they make a "haaah" call that sounds like a
braying donkey.

Galápagos penguins can be quite social creatures, but
when food is scarce, they can be loners. It all depends on

the temperature of the water and the availability of food. When the water is colder, food is plentiful, and the birds can safely feast in large groups of twenty or more. But when the water is warmer and fish are scarce, the penguins eat alone or in pairs.

Like most animals, Galápagos penguins protect their nests and young. Galápagos penguins mate when food is abundant, and breeding can occur all year long, depending upon the available food supply. They lay clutches of two eggs at a time, which can happen as often as three times every fifteen months. Over a period of about five weeks, the parents will take turns staying with the nest or going out to hunt for food. If a predator does threaten the nest, the penguins may defend the area by screeching and pecking. Although laid four days apart, the penguin's eggs might hatch between two and four days apart, but most commonly two days apart. Usually, only one egg survives, which is common among marine birds of the Galápagos.

Threats to the Penguins' Survival

Times are tough for all birds, not just penguins. According to the Worldwatch Institute, an independent environmental organization, more than a thousand species of birds face extinction. Most birds are threatened by human activities, including habitat loss, hunting, pollution, oil spills, and a decline in biological diversity.

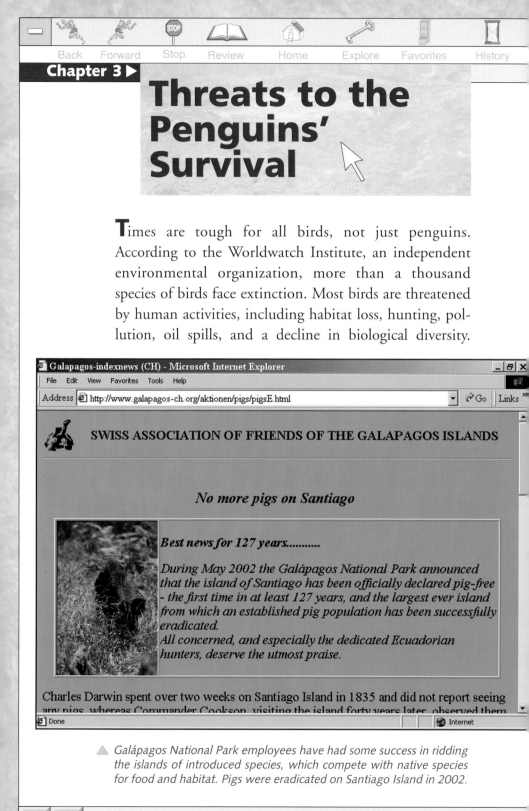

Galapagos-indexnews (CH) - Microsoft Internet Explorer

File Edit View Favorites Tools Help

Address http://www.galapagos-ch.org/aktionen/pigs/pigsE.html Go Links

SWISS ASSOCIATION OF FRIENDS OF THE GALAPAGOS ISLANDS

No more pigs on Santiago

Best news for 127 years...........

During May 2002 the Galápagos National Park announced that the island of Santiago has been officially declared pig-free – the first time in at least 127 years, and the largest ever island from which an established pig population has been successfully eradicated.
All concerned, and especially the dedicated Ecuadorian hunters, deserve the utmost praise.

Charles Darwin spent over two weeks on Santiago Island in 1835 and did not report seeing any pigs, whereas Commander Cookson, visiting the island forty years later, observed them

Done Internet

▲ Galápagos National Park employees have had some success in ridding the islands of introduced species, which compete with native species for food and habitat. Pigs were eradicated on Santiago Island in 2002.

Many of the world's seventeen penguin species are also at risk. The IUCN-World Conservation Union, an international organization of scientists and environmental experts, has included twelve penguin species, including the Galápagos penguin, on its Red List of vulnerable, rare, and endangered animals. Whether they live near the equator or just off Antarctica, penguins are suffering from the same problems as birds everywhere. In the Galápagos, however, the El Niño phenomenon and global climate change—sometimes called "global warming"—are also threats. Although some species are doing well, ". . . Penguins, in general, are experiencing some really serious problems," said Dr. Lloyd Davis, a penguin biologist in New Zealand. "They are in trouble."[1]

Even though 97 percent of the Galápagos Islands has been protected as park area, the islands are still subject to overcrowding, development, and an overabundance of nonnative or "introduced" species, which compete with native species for food and shelter. As a result, many Galápagos animals are at risk, not just penguins. On Santiago Island, introduced pigs had been eating so many of the eggs and hatchlings of native green sea turtles that the species was declining, but since 2001, Galápagos National Park management programs have successfully rid the islands of pigs. At sea, Galápagos sharks have increasingly been killed by illegal industrial fishing or by fishermen who cut off the sharks' prized fins for sale in Asia.

▶ Oil Spills

Oil spills, like that of the tanker *Jessica* in 2001, once posed more of a threat to Galápagos penguins. On the morning of January 16, 2001, a tanker named *Jessica,* on its way to deliver fuel to another ship, crashed into rocky

▲ *Galápagos penguins depend on the waters surrounding the islands for their food. An oil spill could prove disastrous to the penguins and all the marine animals of the Galápagos.*

reefs near the Galápagos Islands, spilling diesel and the much thicker, stickier bunker fuel into the waters off San Cristóbal Island.

The spill soon affected the wildlife for which the Galápagos are famous—killing fish, marine invertebrates, and at least one sea lion. Dozens of iguanas and pelicans had to be cleaned, and other animals were treated for infections from the polluted water. Scientists were especially concerned that the spill would harm the islands' population of endangered Galápagos penguins, either by hurting them directly or by affecting species they depend on for food. Oil destroys the waterproofing quality of a penguin's outer feathers and reduces the air spaces between feathers that help to insulate birds in the water. Species with small populations and limited ranges, such as the Galápagos penguin or the Snares Island penguin, found on just one island south of New Zealand, could be destroyed by a single tanker disaster.

Thankfully, some of the *Jessica*'s spilled diesel fuel evaporated, and the ocean currents carried most of the remaining fuel away from the islands. Local community volunteers joined staff from the Galápagos National Parks Service and the Charles Darwin Research Station to contain the more dangerous bunker fuel as it came close to the coast. They turned over rocks, dug up polluted sand, and ran their hands along coastal trees to make sure no oil had seeped into areas where penguins or other wildlife might live. (The Galápagos penguins nest in holes and crevices in the rocks that lie close to the shore.) Thanks to the efforts of all involved, the penguins were lucky to escape damage during the *Jessica* oil spill. Since that accident, stricter regulations have been put into place, and it is now illegal to bring bunker fuel into the Galápagos Marine Reserve.

"The image of the *Jessica* spewing fuel into this unique environment has dismayed all who value the natural wonders of the world," said Dr. Robert Bensted-Smith, former director of the Charles Darwin Research Station. "Relief that the ecological damage [was not] severe must be accompanied by renewed determination to ensure that the archipelago be protected [forever]."[2]

▷ Changing Temperatures

El Niño weather events come and go every few years in the tropical Pacific Ocean. In El Niño, tropical Pacific Ocean trade winds—west-blowing winds near the equator—die

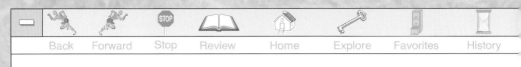
out, and temperatures in the ocean become warmer than usual since colder currents are prevented from moving closer to shore. One effect is that the ocean's surface water remains warmer than usual, killing plankton and driving small fish to greater depths, which affects animals like the Galápagos penguins that depend on the fish for their food. In cooler years, characterized by dry periods known as La Niña, penguin colonies can begin to recover. However, in recent decades, the intensity and frequency of El Niño periods have increased, while the number of La Niña periods has declined—a phenomenon that some scientists believe may be caused by rising global temperatures.

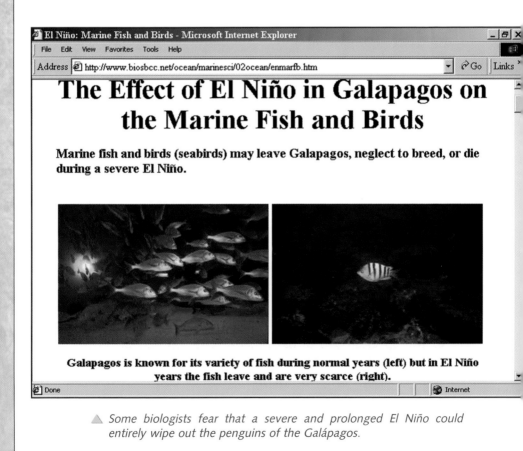

Some biologists fear that a severe and prolonged El Niño could entirely wipe out the penguins of the Galápagos.

In 1998, Dr. Dee Boersma visited the Galápagos to study the effects of a devastating El Niño. There, she saw dead marine iguanas and sea lions and underfed cormorants and penguins. Furthermore, she saw no young penguins, which suggested either that the penguins had not bred in recent months or that chicks did not have enough food to survive. Since 1970, the number of Galápagos penguins had dropped by half, according to Dr. Boersma. Testing the water, she measured temperatures of about 84°F (29°C), which is far too warm to sustain the food supply for penguins and other animals that feed on waterborne creatures. During non-El Niño periods, the waters around the Galápagos can be a full 20 degrees cooler, although the surface temperatures of these waters change depending on the season.

"I'm certainly not at all convinced that the Galápagos penguin is going to go extinct because of this," Dr. Boersma said. "But I am concerned that the numbers are going to become increasingly low, and we know that with smaller populations they're just more vulnerable to extinction."[3]

Toxic Blooms

In recent years, two other South American penguin species, the Magellanic and Humboldt, have also been suffering from changing ocean temperatures caused by El Niño events. Since 1987, the number of Magellanic penguins at Punta Tombo, Argentina, has declined by more than 30 percent. Although hundreds of thousands of penguins still live at Punta Tombo—the largest single colony of this species—the birds are slow to breed and do not begin breeding until they are several years old. Warming temperatures can also lead to the development of waterborne "toxic blooms" that are becoming more frequent and can be deadly to penguins. These blooms involve

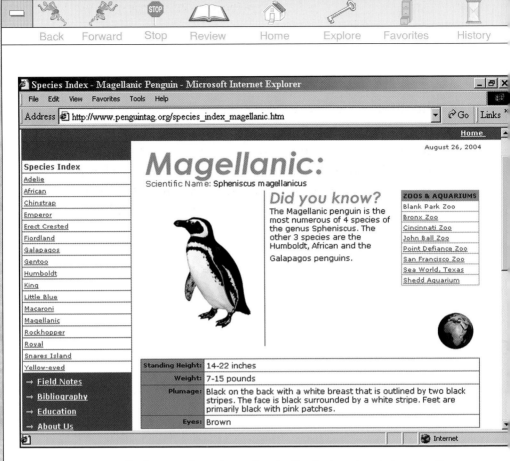

Species Index - Magellanic Penguin - Microsoft Internet Explorer

File Edit View Favorites Tools Help

Address http://www.penguintag.org/species_index_magellanic.htm   Go   Links

Home
August 26, 2004

Species Index
Adelie
African
Chinstrap
Emperor
Erect Crested
Fiordland
Galapagos
Gentoo
Humboldt
King
Little Blue
Macaroni
Magellanic
Rockhopper
Royal
Snares Island
Yellow-eyed
→ **Field Notes**
→ **Bibliography**
→ **Education**
→ **About Us**

Magellanic:
Scientific Name: Spheniscus magellanicus

Did you know?
The Magellanic penguin is the most numerous of 4 species of the genus Spheniscus. The other 3 species are the Humboldt, African and the Galapagos penguins.

ZOOS & AQUARIUMS
Blank Park Zoo
Bronx Zoo
Cincinnati Zoo
John Ball Zoo
Point Defiance Zoo
San Francisco Zoo
Sea World, Texas
Shedd Aquarium

Standing Height:	14-22 inches
Weight:	7-15 pounds
Plumage:	Black on the back with a white breast that is outlined by two black stripes. The face is black surrounded by a white stripe. Feet are primarily black with pink patches.
Eyes:	Brown

Internet

▲ *Magellanic penguins, also native to South America, belong to the same genus,* Spheniscus, *as Galápagos penguins.*

microscopic organisms that reach dangerous levels, or blooms. When these organisms are eaten by fish, and the fish in turn are eaten by larger animals, such as penguins, toxins are concentrated in the animals' tissues, often killing them. In 1990, toxic blooms may have caused the mysterious deaths in New Zealand of more than half of the known population of yellow-eyed penguins. In 2002, thousands of dead and dying Magellanic and gentoo penguins washed up on the shores of the Falkland Islands off Argentina's coast, and scientists think their deaths may also have been caused by a toxic bloom.

▶ Habitat Loss and Hunting

In the last two centuries, human activities have also taken their toll on penguin populations worldwide. In the nineteenth century, millions of penguins throughout the world were killed for their thick layers of fat, which was then rendered into oil, although the Galápagos penguin was not hunted in this way. In the 1870s, for example, the king penguin was completely eliminated from the Falkland Islands, which did not see the return of the species for fifty years. Penguin skins were also once fashionable for leather and trim on women's clothing, and penguin eggs have

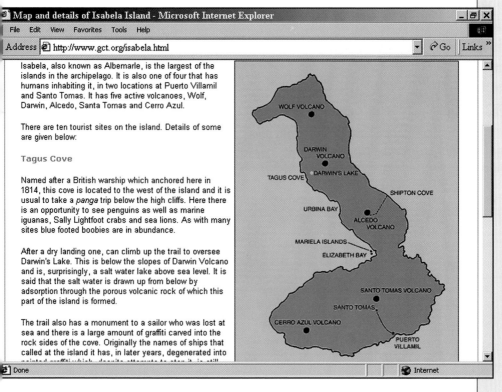

Map and details of Isabela Island - Microsoft Internet Explorer

File   Edit   View   Favorites   Tools   Help

Address 🔗 http://www.gct.org/isabela.html   ⟳ Go   Links »

Isabela, also known as Albemarle, is the largest of the islands in the archipelago. It is also one of four that has humans inhabiting it, in two locations at Puerto Villamil and Santo Tomas. It has five active volcanoes, Wolf, Darwin, Alcedo, Santa Tomas and Cerro Azul.

There are ten tourist sites on the island. Details of some are given below:

Tagus Cove

Named after a British warship which anchored here in 1814, this cove is located to the west of the island and it is usual to take a *panga* trip below the high cliffs. Here there is an opportunity to see penguins as well as marine iguanas, Sally Lightfoot crabs and sea lions. As with many sites blue footed boobies are in abundance.

After a dry landing one, can climb up the trail to oversee Darwin's Lake. This is below the slopes of Darwin Volcano and is, surprisingly, a salt water lake above sea level. It is said that the salt water is drawn up from below by adsorption through the porous volcanic rock of which this part of the island is formed.

The trail also has a monument to a sailor who was lost at sea and there is a large amount of graffiti carved into the rock sides of the cove. Originally the names of ships that called at the island it has, in later years, degenerated into

WOLF VOLCANO

DARWIN VOLCANO
DARWIN'S LAKE
TAGUS COVE
SHIPTON COVE
URBINA BAY
ALCEDO VOLCANO
MARIELA ISLANDS
ELIZABETH BAY
SANTO TOMAS VOLCANO
SANTO TOMAS
CERRO AZUL VOLCANO
PUERTO VILLAMIL

Done   🌐 Internet

▲ A map of Isabela. Isabela and Fernandina are the islands where most Galápagos penguins are found.

been a popular source of food for sailors and settlers. Penguins are still being captured and used for fish bait.

For a long time, the remote Galápagos Islands were sheltered from these sorts of impacts. Yet as tourism and development have increased on the islands, the penguins have become more vulnerable. Isabela and Fernandina islands, the penguins' primary range, were once really popular for illegal fishing. Unlicensed fishermen set up camps, killed giant tortoises for food, and cut down mangrove trees, destroying some of the penguins' prey nursery. For several years, however, the Galápagos National Park Service has regularly patrolled and maintained these areas to stop illegal fishing. Even as they face a dwindling food supply because of waters that lack nutrients and therefore lack fish, penguins have themselves been caught in fishing nets.

▲ Marine iguanas, like Galápagos penguins, have suffered because of the effects of nonnative species that were brought to the islands.

Introduced Species

As more people have come to the islands, they have brought more nonnative animals, including cats, dogs, and rats, that once preyed on native species, including penguin eggs and chicks. These introduced predators have also endangered certain populations of tortoises and iguanas. In the late 1970s, for example, wild dogs killed more than five hundred native iguanas on Santa Cruz Island. In addition, introduced plants have spread quickly and now compete with native vegetation, threatening the food supply for native animals.

Strict park rules now prohibit the introduction of live plants and animals to the island, and cats and dogs are less of a problem today, although black rats remain a threat to the penguins. The Galápagos National Park System has also been involved in successful restoration programs recently. Many captive-bred iguanas and tortoises have been returned to environments with fewer threats to their survival than there were in the past. Park wardens have successfully eliminated goats from six of the islands.

So far, Galápagos National Park officials have not found a completely successful method for dealing with all nonnative animals on the islands. It is difficult to hunt them because the terrain is so rocky. Trapping and poisoning have worked in certain areas, but great care must be taken to make sure that these practices do not also harm native species.

Protection for Penguins

Although people have marveled for centuries at the wildlife found on the Galápagos Islands, efforts to protect the islands' plants and animals have mainly happened in the last fifty years. In the 1930s, the government of Ecuador declared the Galápagos a protected area. In 1959, after three years of investigative trips by UNESCO scientists, the Ecuadorian government created Galápagos National Park, which covers most of the islands. That same year, the Charles Darwin Foundation for the Galápagos Islands was founded under the direction of UNESCO (the United Nations Educational, Scientific, and Cultural Organization) and the IUCN. By 1964, regular research was under way at the foundation's Charles Darwin Research Station, on Santa Cruz Island. In 1978, the islands were named a UNESCO World Heritage Site, a distinction shared by such places as Yellowstone National Park

◀ *Penguins preen their feathers frequently to keep them waterproof.*

in the United States, the Tower of London in England, and the Great Wall of China. Places that receive World Heritage status can also receive special attention and protection if threatened.

An Uneasy Living Arrangement

Yet, research and conservation efforts have come under fire from island residents. The island of Santa Cruz, home to the Charles Darwin Research Station and the headquarters of Galápagos National Park, is also home to Puerto Ayora, the largest town in all the islands, which includes hotels, shops, and restaurants. Conservationists and locals often disagree about how human activities should be managed to protect Galápagos wildlife. Local fishermen and business owners say that the conservation regulations are too restrictive. Sometimes, clashes between residents and conservationists have turned violent.

Despite these challenges, conservation groups and government officials have worked hard to protect the islands' penguins and other native species. The Special Law of 1998 provides the legal and political framework for long-term management. And in many places in the world, recent decades have seen the rise of a "conservation conscience," as bird expert Roger Tory Peterson has written.[1]

Galápagos National Park

Galápagos National Park provides protection for the islands' Galápagos penguins. The park is managed by the Galápagos National Park Service, a government agency that is dedicated to protecting both the ecosystems of the archipelago and their biological diversity.

Maintaining offices on Santa Cruz, Floreana, Isabela, and San Cristóbal islands, the park service works specifically

▲ *The Galápagos National Park Service has one of its offices on Floreana Island, pictured. This island, an active volcano, is also one of the oldest: Geologists have found its lava flows date from 1.5 million years ago.*

to protect penguins and other sensitive Galápagos animals from threats including tourism, introduced species, fishing, and agricultural development. The park service also works with universities to monitor species and continually patrols the islands by land, sea, and air. The Galápagos National Park Service also works with the Charles Darwin Research Station and other conservation organizations.

Perhaps most important, the park service helps to enforce the Special Law for the Galápagos, which has been called the Ecuadorian government's strongest commitment to island conservation. This law restricted migration to the islands, created the more-than 50,000-square-mile (129,500-square-kilometer) Galápagos Marine Reserve, and increased funding for the park service. After decades in which different parts of the islands were managed in different ways, the Special Law also required that the Galápagos be managed in a way that covers the whole archipelago, including the national park, marine reserve, and developed areas.

In 1999, because of the Special Law, Ecuadorian officials created the System of Inspection and Quarantine for the Galápagos. This measure has been critical in curbing the introduction of nonnative species through the islands' ports and airports.

Bird-Watching

Since the seventeenth century, about 93 percent of all bird extinctions in the world have been island species, according to the Charles Darwin Research Station.[2] So far, no Galápagos bird species has gone extinct, although localized colonies of certain species have disappeared. The station has identified a total of 140 species of birds on the islands: 58 species that live there all year long, 76 migratory species, and 6 nonnative species.[3] Research has shown that human activities, natural events, and introduced wildlife pose the greatest threats to native birds.

Protection of the Galápagos penguins begins with accurate information on their population numbers, breeding locations, and mortality rates. This information is gathered by the scientists and volunteers at the Charles Darwin Research Station, whose work is funded through the support of its donors. Because there is strength in numbers, most conservation groups focused on the Galápagos willingly work with other groups to monitor native bird species. The Galápagos Conservation Trust, for example, is affiliated with an international network known as the Friends of Galápagos, which includes groups in the United States, Canada, Germany, Switzerland, the Netherlands, and Spain. It has made protection of island birds a special focus. SeaWorld currently funds a great deal of the research done on the Galápagos penguin.

Since 1970, the Charles Darwin Research Station and the Galápagos National Park Service have also conducted annual censuses, targeting penguins and flightless cormorants. These surveys help to evaluate population changes caused by human activities and natural events such as El Niño. In 1999, for example, the census observed several penguin nests with eggs and chicks,

▲ A rocky coast of the Galápagos teems with marine life that includes a Galápagos penguin at rest, some marine iguanas, and colorful Sally Lightfoot crabs.

▲ *Galápagos penguins are fast and agile swimmers, reaching speeds of up to 24 miles per hour (39 kilometers per hour).*

which indicated that the penguin population had recovered somewhat from the major El Niño event the year before. The station has also conducted special projects to determine how introduced species, such as rats, and bird diseases such as avian pox, affect penguins and other native birds.

In 2003, the research station performed its annual survey of Galápagos penguins and made a distressing discovery. The study counted only 770 penguins, down from 848 in 2002. Monitoring is not enough to protect this sensitive species from extinction, however. Scientists who study penguins stress that it is only by dealing with threats to their survival that the Galápagos penguin can be truly protected.

Survival of the Flightless

Ever since humans first stumbled across these strange, isolated islands, the Galápagos have been called by several different names. The islands are formally known as the *Archipelago de Colon,* named for the Italian explorer Christopher Columbus, whose name in Spanish was *Cristóbal Colón.* Tomás de Berlanga called the Galápagos *Las Encantadas,* "the Enchanted Isles."

Today, so many tourists find the islands enchanting that their presence is threatening the very plants and wildlife that people go there to see. In 2003, according to one estimate, about 92,000 visitors came to the islands, arriving by planes, private jets, and private yachts. To control the impacts of tourism, the Galápagos National Park has placed quotas, or strict limits, on the number of tourists that can visit the islands. That limit angers some local residents, who believe that increasing tourism would help to support small businesses.

In March 2004, visitors to the Galápagos witnessed a tense standoff in Puerto Ayora between local fishermen and the Charles Darwin Research Station. The fishermen, who were protesting restrictions on fishing, blocked the station for a week. They even threatened to kill a famous giant tortoise—named Lonesome George—if their demands were not met. Violence was avoided when fishermen and the Ecuadorian government agreed to develop a commission to study the fishing regulations, and the protest ended with no injuries to people or wildlife.

▲ *Although tourism is important to the economy of Ecuador's Galápagos Islands, its impact on the islands' wildlife worries many conservationists.*

Unfortunately, only three months later, fishermen on Isabela occupied a national park office and interrupted tour boat arrivals in a continuation of their protest over restrictions on fishing.[1] Some conservationists question whether fishing should be allowed at all in the Galápagos. The struggle between the rights of the people on these islands versus those of the native wildlife continues.

▶ High-Tech Monitoring

In recent years, scientists at the Charles Darwin Research Station have turned to more advanced technology to help collect data on native birds. In 1998, the station began using the Global Positioning System, or GPS, a navigational system that uses satellite signals to fix upon a location on Earth, in their monitoring work. GPS allows the transmission of data to portable computers. That data can then be transferred later into a Geographic Information System (GIS) at the station. GIS uses computerized databases and maps that allow the analysis of data from several different points of view. This system is a powerful tool, station scientists say, for "ecological analysis, used towards the restoration of native bird populations."[2]

The research station also monitors native birds using more traditional methods. For example, naturalist-guides have provided observations to scientists about penguins, lava gulls, flamingos, cormorants, frigate birds, and boobies. As guides travel to the same sites each week, their information helps researchers track trends of bird activities, populations, and reproduction rates.

A Species Protection Project

In 2003, a new multiyear research project on the Galápagos penguin was announced. Through 2006, the project team will conduct scientific research into the effects of climate change, introduced predators, and fisheries on the penguin and two other endangered bird species native to the Galápagos—the mangrove finch and the flightless cormorant. The project will focus on the western coast of the Galápagos, home to 95 percent of Galápagos penguin populations, 98 percent of mangrove finch colonies, and all of the flightless cormorant populations.

Researchers hope that their work will help to develop scientifically based management plans to protect those species and further reduce the threats to their survival. To do this, the project team will install monitoring devices at several locations in the western part of the archipelago and tag about one third of the three bird populations. The data produced from this monitoring will be studied along with information about seawater temperatures and precipitation. That information will help to determine the impacts of major weather events on these endangered species.

▷ Predicting El Niño

One of the key factors that the team will be studying is how El Niño weather events harm endangered species— and also how they might help. As recent events have shown, El Niño can certainly reduce the populations of Galápagos penguins and other marine species by making fragile populations even more vulnerable to predators and starvation because of competition for food. However, wet El Niño periods actually help land species such as the mangrove finch by increasing the availability of the specific

plants or invertebrates that finches feed on. These finches actually suffer population drops during the colder La Niña periods that allow penguins to recover.

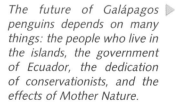

The future of Galápagos ▷ penguins depends on many things: the people who live in the islands, the government of Ecuador, the dedication of conservationists, and the effects of Mother Nature.

The species protection project is designed to help park managers make predictions on which populations will be affected by El Niño events and how. Because changing precipitation levels and sea surface temperatures are both good indicators of a coming El Niño, the project will test how much these two factors can predict bird population changes.

Hope for the Future

When the species protection project is completed, the team hopes to create an electronic database to track data on penguins and other birds. Multilayered maps of the data will be produced by using the existing GIS at the Charles Darwin Research Station. At least eight Ecuadorian students will be trained in research methods and conservation biology, and eight park managers will be trained in wildlife management and monitoring techniques.

"This is a unique and innovative project that will certainly benefit the local people and have a long-term positive effect on biodiversity conservation in Galápagos," said Hernan Vargas, a Galápagos-born biologist who developed the project and now heads the Ornithology (Bird) Department of the Charles Darwin Research Station.[3]

Right now, it is too soon to tell whether these and other conservation efforts will be enough to save the Galápagos penguin. But they offer the species its best hope for recovery. As Charles Darwin wrote more than 140 years ago, "The vigorous, the healthy, and the happy survive and multiply."[4] Thanks to the conservation work on the islands and the support of many organizations, this statement may once again be true of the rare Galápagos penguins.

The Endangered and Threatened Wildlife List

This series is based on the Endangered and Threatened Wildlife list compiled by the U.S. Fish and Wildlife Service (USFWS). Each book explores an endangered or threatened animal, tells why it has become endangered or threatened, and explains the efforts being made to restore the species' population.

The United States Fish and Wildlife Service, in the Department of the Interior, and the National Marine Fisheries Service, in the Department of Commerce, share responsibility for administration of the Endangered Species Act.

In 1973, Congress took the farsighted step of creating the Endangered Species Act, widely regarded as the world's strongest and most effective wildlife conservation law. It set an ambitious goal: to reverse the alarming trend of human-caused extinction that threatened the ecosystems we all share.

The complete list of Endangered and Threatened Wildlife and Plants can be found at **http://endangered.fws.gov/wildlife.html#Species.**

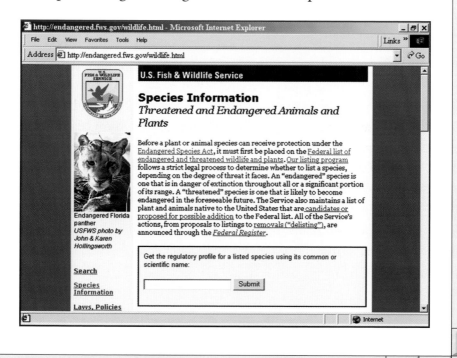

Chapter 1. Penguins—and an Island Paradise—at Risk
1. Les Line, "Into the Abyss?" *International Wildlife,* vol. 27, no. 5, September 19, 1997, p. 12.

Chapter 2. Island Natives: Special Characteristics
1. Galapagos Conservation Trust, "Charles Darwin," n.d., <www.gct.org/darwin.html> (May 20, 2004).

Chapter 3. Threats to the Penguins' Survival
1. Carol Kaesuk Yoon, "Penguins in Trouble Worldwide," *The New York Times,* June 26, 2001, p. F1.

2. World Wildlife Fund, "Galápagos under Siege: Oil Spill 2001," n.d., <www.worldwildlife.org/galapagos/spill.cfm> (May 20, 2004).

3. CNN.com, Environmental News Network, "El Niño takes its toll on penguins," May 29, 1998, <www.cnn.com/TECH/science/9805/29/el.nino.penguins> (May 20, 2004).

Chapter 4. Protection for Penguins
1. Roger Tory Peterson, *Penguins* (Boston: Houghton Mifflin, 1979), p. 222.

2. The Charles Darwin Foundation for the Galapagos Islands, The Charles Darwin Research Station, "The Ornithology Program of the Charles Darwin Research Station," n.d., <http://www.darwinfoundation.org/terrest/birds.html> (May 19, 2004).

3. Ibid.

Chapter 5. Survival of the Flightless
1. The Charles Darwin Foundation, Inc., "Another Fishery Protest Underway in Galapagos," June 4, 2004, <http://www.galapagos.org/whatsnew/fishermen060404.html> (August 25, 2004).

2. The Charles Darwin Foundation for the Galapagos Islands, The Charles Darwin Research Station, "Ornithology, Censuses, and Monitoring of Birds," n.d., <http://www.darwinfoundation.org/terrest/census.html> (August 11, 2004).

3. Galapagos Conservation Trust, "Darwin Initiative awards grant to project on climate change and the conservation of Galapagos endemic bird species," n.d., <www.gct.org/apr03_3.html> (May 20, 2004).

4. Charles Darwin, *On the Origin of Species: A Facsimile of the First Edition* (Cambridge, Mass.: Harvard University Press, 1975), p. 79.

Further Reading

Chester, Jonathan. *The Nature of Penguins.* Berkeley, Calif.: Celestial Arts, 2001.

Daniels, Amy S. *Ecuador.* Milwaukee: Gareth Stevens Publishing, 2002.

Lynch, Wayne. *Penguins!* Toronto: Firefly Books, 1999.

Pascoe, Elaine, ed. *Into the Galapagos.* San Diego: Blackbirch Press, 2004.

Penny, Malcolm. *Endangered Species: Our Impact on the Planet.* Austin, Tex.: Raintree Steck-Vaughn Publishers, 2002.

Sayre, April Pulley. *El Niño and La Niña: Weather in the Headlines.* Brookfield, Conn.: Twenty-First Century Books, 2000.

Sis, Peter. *The Tree of Life.* New York: Farrar Straus Giroux, 2003.

Spilsbury, Louise, and Richard Spilsbury. *A Rookery of Penguins.* Chicago: Heinemann Library, 2004.

Steadman, David W., and Steven Zousmer. *Galápagos: Discovery on Darwin's Islands.* Washington, D.C.: Smithsonian Institution Press, 1988.

Tagilaferro, Linda. *Galápagos Islands: Nature's Delicate Balance at Risk.* Minneapolis: Lerner Publishing, 2001.

Webb, Sophie. *My Season With Penguins: An Antarctic Journal.* Boston: Houghton Mifflin, 2000.

Index